DIVA
UNLEASHED

*Embracing your Worth with
Determination, Intelligence,
Victory and Angelic Grace*

DIVA
UNLEASHED

Embracing your Worth with Determination, Intelligence, Victory and Angelic Grace

ROSE ROBERTSON

Foreword by Thomas Robertson III

Copyright © 2024 Rose Robertson.

T&R Publishing

All rights reserved. No part of this book may be reproduced or used in any manner without written permission from the publisher, except by a reviewer who may quote brief passages in a review with appropriate credits; nor may any part of this book be reproduced, stored in a retrieval system, or transmitted in any form or by any means—electronic, mechanical, photocopying, recording, or other—without written permission from the publisher.

Printed in the United States of America

First Printing, 2024

ISBN: 979-8-218-48391-3 (paperback)
ISBN: 979-8-218-48392-0 (ebook)

Rose Robertson
P.O. Box 1054
Rex, Ga 30273

DEDICATION

I dedicate this book to all the women
who have faced challenges and felt
the weight of the world on their shoulders, this
book is for you. May it serve
as a reminder that no matter what you go
through, you are strong, resilient,
and worthy. Never lose sight of your value, and
always remember—you matter.

CONTENTS

Foreword . . . . **xi**
    Supporting Your Queen xi

Chapter 1: Awakening to Purpose **1**
    Affirm DIVA! 1
    Stop: 5
    Start: 5
    Reflective Exercise 7

Chapter 2: The D.I.V.A. Mindset **9**
    Affirm DIVA! 9
    Stop: 15
    Start: 16
    Reflective Exercise 17

Chapter 3: Balancing Act: Juggling Hats **19**
    Affirm DIVA! 19
    Stop: 24

    Start: 25
    Reflective Exercise 26

Chapter 4: Claiming Your Worth 29
    Affirm DIVA! 29
    Stop: 35
    Start: 36
    Reflective Exercise 37

Chapter 5: Leading with Purpose 39
    Affirm DIVA! 39
    Stop: 41
    Start: 42
    Reflective Exercise 43

Chapter 6: Navigating Challenges 45
    Affirm DIVA! 45
    Stop: 47
    Start: 48
    Reflective Exercise 49

Chapter 7: Empowering Others 51
    Affirm DIVA! 51
    Stop: 53
    Start: 54
    Reflective Exercise 55

Chapter 8: Embracing Self-Care............57
Affirm DIVA! 57
Stop: 59
Start: 60
Reflective Exercise 61

Chapter 9: Finding Purpose in Pain 63
Affirm DIVA! 63
Stop: 65
Start: 66
Reflective Exercise 67

Chapter 10: Embracing Your Testimony 69
Affirm DIVA! 69
Stop: 71
Start: 72
Reflective Exercise 73

Acknowledgments......................75

Foreword

Supporting Your Queen

As I woke up on Christmas morning, like any other morning, I checked to see if my wife was still asleep. She was awake but had this strange look. It wasn't a look of pain, which confused me at the time; it was just an odd look. I asked if everything was okay, and she said yes. She was thinking about something that had come to her in her sleep: knowing her worth. I questioned myself, and asked her if she thought about her worth with me and whether she felt that she sometimes had to look outside the box. As she lay there, she said she had a dream about herself, about where she was in life, and knowing her worth. As I lay there, I thought maybe she was wondering about her gift or the blessing of seeing another Christmas. I was thinking about my gift and my pancakes and eggs, and also, starting to think about my worth as a husband to her and as a father to our kids. And so, we continued our fascinating conversation about knowing one's worth.

As husbands, we often shoulder the responsibility of providing for our families, ensuring that bills are paid and needs are met. Yet, in the hustle and bustle of daily life, do we show our wives the appreciation they deserve? Do we demonstrate to them their immeasurable worth in our lives?

It's easy to get caught up in the routine and become so focused on external obligations that we overlook the importance of nurturing the bond with our life partners. But if we take a moment to reflect on our relationships, we realize that it's the simple gestures that matter most to our wives. They don't ask for grand gestures or extravagant displays of affection; they truly desire our genuine presence and support.

As men, we often carry the world's weight on our shoulders, striving to maintain an image of strength and stoicism. Yet, beneath the surface, we, too, crave understanding, companionship, and acceptance. We may feel the pressure to conform to societal expectations of masculinity, but deep down, we yearn for the freedom to express our true selves without fear of judgment or ridicule.

It's time to let down our guard, embrace vulnerability, and show our wives the multifaceted individuals we are. Let's set aside the facade of invincibility and allow ourselves to be silly, sensitive, and sincere. Let's create a safe space where open communication and mutual respect thrive, where we can share our joys and struggles without reservation.

Let's redefine what it means to be a supportive partner, a faithful companion who uplifts and empowers their spouse to reach their full potential. Let's celebrate each other's strengths and champion each other's dreams, knowing that our worth lies not in the roles we fulfill but in the love and acceptance we offer unconditionally.

So, my fellow kings, let's stand tall in our roles as husbands, fathers, and leaders but let's also recognize the importance of being allies and advocates for our queens. Let's affirm their beauty, intelligence, and resilience at every turn, reminding them they are cherished, valued, and deeply loved.

By embracing our roles as supportive partners, we uplift our wives and enrich our own lives immeasurably. Together, let's embark on this journey of self-discovery and mutual appreciation, knowing that as partners, we are stronger, wiser, and more fulfilled than we could ever be alone.

Enjoy the read,
Thomas Robertson III

CHAPTER 1

Awakening to Purpose

Affirm DIVA!
"I am worthy of all the love, success, and happiness that life has to offer. Today, I embrace my true worth and take steps toward my purpose with confidence and clarity."

I'm up all night tossing and turning, my mind constantly racing. I wear many hats, so I usually try to prepare myself for the next day ahead of time. I have to balance my personal and business life so as not to fall short somewhere, which, of course, I feel I do at times. And well, on this particular morning—Christmas Day—I was awakened by a voice at 5:23 a.m. saying to me, "Know Your Worth." I had been fasting and praying, and asking God to lead me to my next assignment. Of course, I immediately got up, went to my office, and started writing down what God had just said. While moving around, my hubby asked if I was okay. I replied, "Yes, I just needed to go to my office for a minute to write something down." While sitting at my desk, I smiled, telling myself that this was it. I had been struggling for some time with so many obstacles coming at me that I could not get a hold of. I knew I could do so much better, but I struggled with and juggled so many things to make it through the day. I had started questioning who I was and the decisions I was making. Even though I felt they were the right ones, I still caught myself doubting myself more and more. I walked around as if I was okay, but inside, I was mentally tired of fighting to get my points across, both in business and personally. It seemed as if every time I said something, no matter who I was communicating with, it somehow ended up not quite in a debate but in being forced to explain myself excessively to help people understand what I was saying. Of course, I started to feel like maybe I was not communicating effectively, so I started changing how I would say things. I wrote down what I heard and some other notes and returned to bed. Shortly after I returned to bed, my hubby and I went ahead and got up for the day, realizing we had a long day ahead of us. We had plans for family and friends to come over. He asked what was going on with me and why I got up in such a hurry earlier. I replied that I finally knew what I'd been missing, what I'd been lacking. He looked at me strangely and asked what it was. I explained to him that I was woken up by a voice saying, "Know Your Worth."

He smiled and told me we should realize our worth in everything we do.

We smiled at each other and prepared for our day. While talking about our plans, I reached out to all the kids and realized one of them wasn't doing so well. We turned to each other and knew that this was the ENEMY attempting to step in. We immediately decided to bring him home for the holiday so we could make sure he was in the presence of family to take care of him. After, we prayed and continued with our day. Of course, everyone was waiting for me to cook our Christmas meal, which we ate as we laughed, talked, and played games throughout the day. We took time to remember our family and loved ones who weren't able to be with us on Christmas Day but we thanked God for all the obstacles he brought us through and his many blessings. Then, as if our morning wasn't interrupted enough, we ended our evening with another child involved in a situation that could have cost him his life. Still, God is always bringing us through.

Understand why hearing God say, "Know Your Worth" is essential to me.

I felt like I was starting to lose myself while I was worrying about everyone and everything else. Even though I would always hear, "It's all about Rose," even though none of my decisions were ever what was best for me, I still seemed to do what was best for others. I was always asking about and making sure everyone else was good, but after that night, I started asking myself, "Who is making sure Rose is good? What if I need someone to listen to me, to take the lead instead of waiting for me to do it? To do anything, for once?"

In my despair, I had to remind myself that I was human. I can be a mother, wife, grandmother, author, CEO, boss, or whatever I need to be, but where was the time for me? I've realized that people don't seem to recognize how much I do. But I don't make the rules, I enforce them. And when you enforce rules, no matter what your title is, people always tend to take the positive and somehow turn it into a negative, always out to make you the bad person. Overall, through all the juggling of my responsibilities, if I don't have ME, what good am I to anyone else?

Each day, we continue to learn more and more about ourselves. We take what we see and we use it to better ourselves. But amid everything, we forget to stop living for everybody else. You have to live for YOU. Stop worrying about who likes you and why they don't agree with you or talk to you. Stop putting off what you've been wanting to accomplish. Start your business, write your book. Be self-motivated and surround yourself with people who will motivate you and push you to succeed with your goals.

Take ownership of whatever you're involved with; you lead and control the situation. It's yours until you release it. As a part of my routine, I have programmed myself to write my thoughts and what I want to do in my agendas daily. Try it and use your agenda for what you've assigned yourself to do for that season. Be sure to complete the assignment before moving on to the next one. Nothing can be left undone if we want to reach our goals. Keep your standards high; there's no limit to what we can do. Claim and get to know yourself again; you are your biggest supporter. Remember, God sees us during the mess we've made. But in the end, he'll always turn our mess into our testimony.

Stop:

- Ignoring your inner thoughts; honor your intuition and listen to the guidance from within. Acknowledge its validity and importance in your decision-making process.
- Second-guessing what you can do; release self-doubt and trust in your abilities. When you believe in yourself, you are capable of achieving great things.
- Allowing people to control you; set healthy boundaries and assert your autonomy. Refuse to let others dictate your actions or define your worth.

Start:

- Trusting your thoughts; embrace your inner wisdom and the insights that arise within you. Recognize them as valuable guidance on your life's journey.

- Motivating yourself; cultivate a mindset of self-motivation and empowerment. Inspire yourself to take action toward your goals and dreams with determination and enthusiasm.
- Putting you first; prioritize your well-being and aspirations. Honor your needs, desires, and self-care practices as essential components of a fulfilling and balanced life.

Reflective Exercise

Reflect on a moment when you felt a profound clarity about your life's purpose. What triggered this awakening? How did this realization impact your actions and mindset? Write about how embracing your worth has changed how you navigate your personal and professional life.

CHAPTER 2

The D.I.V.A. Mindset

Affirm DIVA!

"I am a D.I.V.A.: Determined, Intelligent, Victorious, and Angelic. I embrace my inner strength, face challenges head-on, and rise above them gracefully and confidently."

From early on, even until now, I have challenged myself regularly to make sure I continue to push and better myself. Others look at my success, and think that I feel I am above them. But they do not know my total story, nor the obstacles and challenges that placed me where I am now. It may be hard to do, because we focus so heavily on outside comments and dissect each other, but a D.I.V.A. never lets another individual stop what they've set out to accomplish. Your accomplishments come from your hard work and dedication. No one knows the long days and nights of not sleeping, trying to see how this and that is going to happen to be able to succeed. The only thing they see is what's in front of them or what they assume.

I truly feel we all should be there for one another to motivate and hold each other accountable. In the end, we all have the same goal, and that is to succeed at whatever we are trying to do. Often, I think of this young lady who didn't care for me and gave me the most challenging time when we communicated. No matter what I said, she had to come back at me quickly. One day, I asked her why she didn't receive what I said to her when she asked for my opinion or advice. Her reply was, "Mrs. Rose, honestly, I admire you. I see what I miss in my mom in you." She said she listens to everything I say and uses it to the best of her knowledge, but that she envied me for some time, wondering how I can be so strong when I have so much on me. I replied, "I'm not always strong; I handle things as they come, one thing at a time."

I do what I can do when I can, and whatever's left will wait until I have the time to do it. We laughed, and she replied, "Remember Mrs. Rose, you always say "Make It Happen." I encourage myself and others with those words. I tell them, "Let's Make It Happen." By no means is it easy when someone is always watching. Somehow, the ones that seem to be motivating you or motivated by you can also be the ones working against you. Regardless of their choice, remember to worry only about what's best for you and what you have set yourself up to accomplish. Leave the world outside your comfort zone and let them be. Everyone will not see your dreams and visions as you do; therefore, they will not understand what you are working toward.

I feel I was and still am very different from many other women. I grew up seeing my mom working hard to make sure ends met. Yes, my father was there, but my mom was my role model. As a woman, she worked so hard with the many things she did, making sure we were taken care of and that you had to help your mate make things happen within the home. With me, I started having kids at a young age, which I wouldn't change for anything. We grew up together, which was very hard but enjoyable at the same time. No, I'm not promoting teen pregnancy; I'm only acknowledging what I did. Being a teen Mom had its struggles, from trying to grow into motherhood while still learning myself to learning how to raise more than one child. And, of course, how to discipline a child with me being so young. Because of that, and being around unsupportive people, I used to second-guess myself. I was uncomfortable and embarrassed, but I finally forgave myself and moved on. I finally accepted it. I couldn't change what I did now that I had kids, but I could make sure I was there for my kids and that I took care of my kids. I told myself way back then that I would never allow my kids to refer to my mom as their mother like so many young women did. I accepted that my life had to change to do what was best for my kids now. I started working at a young age to ensure I could meet all financial obligations to care for my kids. While working at night while I was pregnant and doing braids during the day and weekends, I was finally blessed to find and work a regular job and start my career path. My road during that time wasn't always easy, being a young mom and never having time and a personal life. I think back to when I was a kid, and once I was older and had my kids, I thought I lived my childhood through them. We spent many weekends skating and at the movies, so I could not only give them things to do, but that was my outlet to relax my mind and not always be thinking about my many obligations.

People look at me now and say, "You don't know what it means to struggle." I giggle and shake my head, knowing there were several times I made sure my kids ate even if I didn't eat. I kept food in the house and all bills paid by myself. I kept the mindset of NOT allowing my parents to be my kid's parents. I made sure I was the parent, and I made ends meet. I look back now and see that even at a young age, I knew what I needed to do. I knew I had to push and grind daily, but I didn't understand my WORTH. Now that I'm older, I see it in my kids who push toward their dreams and ensure they make things happen every day. I tried to stay strong, not showing them my pain even when I didn't know how things would get done, not knowing if not showing them was a good or a bad thing. Even at a young age, and being at my lowest point many times. I cried myself to sleep many nights, worried, of course, but I continued to keep my bible close, and I made sure I stayed in prayer, and somehow, things always came together for my good.

Yes, I've been there and done that. I look back over decades of my life and smile to see that I've made it through significant challenges. I've been labeled as so many disrespectful things, which for a long time I let bother me mentally, but I finally grew to understand that some people's words can be cruel and mean but mainly hurt inside themselves. Therefore, they lash out to cover up their pain. I used to smile on the outside but cry within, saying to myself, "If only they would take the time to get to know "ROSE," they might even love her. I can now smile and maintain it, knowing it's now my genuine smile that I've earned without any regrets, no matter who feels whatever way they do about me. I've learned to start counting to ten in my mind, which gives me time to process and think before speaking. I tell myself that I'm not here to match anyone's energy; I'm here to maintain a positive environment and stay focused on the direction I need to go.

D.I.V.A., it's okay. Let go of the hurt and the worry and keep your SMILE. I lived a shielded life. I didn't fit in, maybe because back then and even now, I'm about making sure I don't hang with the wrong people or make decisions based on trends just to fit in. Take a minute or two and think about that. Some individuals need to be the center of attention, you and I want to be behind the scenes, MAKING THINGS HAPPEN. Whenever you see anyone constantly trying to be seen, it's not always for the right reason. Sometimes, it is for attention—for all the wrong reasons. We have to realize no matter what their reasonings are, it has nothing to do with us. It's something that one has to accept and deal with. I even catch myself staying away from crowds, feeling like I didn't and don't belong. But I'm finally realizing, even if my credentials and my goals are different from others, we are all the same. What people don't want to accept is that when you don't want negative spirits on you, you don't involve yourself around it. I push and push and ask myself how I can make it daily, and my answer always seems to come back to MY GOD. My mind is always racing with things. While sitting here, I am thinking about what I will write next. I took a break and put on some worship music, one of my outlets, to help me relax. While I was listening to the radio, they asked, "Are you looking through the right lens?" I didn't understand the question at first, but then I sat with it. You already know what my answer was: NO, NO, NO. Going through my memories, I realized I was trying to fit in with people who mean me no good, and I just continued to turn my head to things they do that I knew I should walk away from. Things that weren't right for me or for me to be around. So many of us do this regularly, just figuring that it'll be okay, it won't hurt us.

Things improve when we live according to what's best for ourselves rather than others. I've learned to set boundaries and engage with people on my terms, not out of obligation. Your terms don't mean only when it benefits you or when you get something out of it, your terms mean when you have the time, or when it won't harm your spirit to make yourself available for that person. We must accept that we all have good and bad things about us, which is why we are all different but the same in many ways. We cannot change a person, but we don't have to associate ourselves with that person. We can love and respect them but we never have to allow them into our personal space. We must remember that no matter how bad we think our storm is, it's only God's way of preparing us for the sunshine, "Our Testimony." Stop looking back. Take that next step, that leap of faith. We can continue to go on and on, but the past only gets further and further behind us. We must stop allowing it to affect our future. Stop letting our situations make us doubt ourselves. We can have anything we put our minds to. Take that next step toward what's best for you, not what's best for family and friends, for which there's no guarantee that they will be there for you anyway. Learn how to love yourself, trust in your abilities, and depend on YOU to make your own decisions.

Stop:

- Allowing the outside to control your mindset. Take ownership of your thoughts and emotions, and recognize that you can cultivate a positive and empowered mindset independent of external circumstances.

- Listening to others' negative comments. Guard your mental space against negativity by filtering out harmful remarks and focusing on uplifting and supportive influences that nurture your growth.
- Living in the past, the future is where our world begins. Release the grip of past regrets or future anxieties and anchor yourself in the present moment, where opportunities for growth and transformation are abound.

Start:

- Removing the clutter from your mind: Engage in mindfulness practices, journaling, or meditation to declutter your thoughts and create mental space for clarity and focus.
- Challenging yourself to Set ambitious yet attainable goals that stretch your capabilities and inspire personal growth, fostering a mindset of continuous improvement and achievement.
- Working toward your goals: Take consistent action toward your aspirations, breaking them down into manageable steps and staying committed to your journey of progress and fulfillment.

Reflective Exercise

Reflect on a time when you embodied the D.I.V.A. mindset. Describe a specific challenge and how you overcame it with determination, intelligence, a victorious attitude, and a compassionate heart. How did this experience shape your self-perception and influence your future actions? Embracing these qualities will help you achieve personal fulfillment and navigate life's obstacles.

___

___

___

___

___

___

___

___

___

___

___

___

CHAPTER 3

Balancing Act: Juggling Hats

Affirm DIVA!

"I am a balance master, wearing each hat gracefully and determinedly. I honor my responsibilities while nurturing my well-being, knowing I am capable and resilient."

As women, we must juggle many hats to ensure we can get through our day. Many of us have to jump into being mothers and wives, getting things ready, making breakfast or lunch, or whatever our morning routine requires. Some hats are simple to wear, and others are more complex. Some only take up short periods of time while others are long. In our day-to-day life, we push ourselves as far as we can go, not allowing the world to see our struggles. It is not easy at all, but I, along with many other women, do not allow these struggles to determine who I am. As hard as it may be, I've learned how to multitask, and how to wear one or two hats at a time.

For example, mothers like me want what's best for our kids. Each mother has different thoughts and solutions on what exactly that means, but we do what we think is right. So many mothers choose to make decisions that lead to the wrong outcomes, but does that make them bad? No, that mother just chose what she thought was suitable for that particular moment and situation, and she owes no one an explanation. As mothers, we protect our kids from any wrongdoings, watch them grow into adulthood, and pray they will learn the right life lessons and make the right decisions. As they grow, life happens, and when it does, we cannot continue to blame ourselves for the decisions our children make. We can only accept that we raised them to the best of our ability and pray that they allow Jesus Christ in their life. Yes, it's easy to say this, but when reality hits, it's hard for a mother when something is not going right for her kids or when a mother and her children are not agreeing on something together. When we are aware of things they are going through, we don't sleep and worry for days until we know their decision has worked itself out. I listen to some of the stories my children tell now, and find that I don't remember or I know nothing about them. Learning so late that certain things happened makes me a little upset, and I would have handled some situations differently, but we should realize that some of our decisions may have influenced our children's choices. We can assume and continue to try to figure it out, but we cannot change those decisions now. We can only assist them if and when they allow us to help or when they ask for advice. We must thank God for stepping in and covering them again through their storm. We would never allow them to grow up if it was up to us. They would always remain our babies, with us guiding their lives every step and every day.

Women, let's stop worrying about and looking down on the lives of other mothers when we have no idea of the details. We must stop speaking negatively about another mother when we should be lifting her up and helping her through whatever her challenge may be at that time. If a mother comes to you for assistance and you feel you don't have the means, then say just that. Don't take her situation and run with it, discussing it for your pleasure. Let's work on having positive conversations with our sisters. The world alone gives her enough negativity to fight through daily.

As wives, we tend to carry more on our shoulders than we realize due to our heavy daily routines becoming normal. Wives take on the role of cleaning, cooking, spending quality time with their husbands, making sure the bills are physically paid, and many more things regularly. But, during all of this, we cannot lose ourselves. We must take time out to still do what we need to do for ourselves, whether it's a long bubble bath, reading a book, getting nails and hair done, shopping, and more. That time is time for us to reset and re-focus.

We're the wife, not the maid, chef, financial advisor, or counselor. As a wife, we will make mistakes or fall short sometimes. Ladies, we will even stand by our spouses when they make mistakes, which is okay, but are they learning from them? Their mistakes are their mistakes. Don't make it your mistake. Do you find yourself making excuses for your spouse? Maybe if I had done _____, he wouldn't have done _____. I should do _____, then he might not do _____. Suppose you continued to stay with him after his mistake. In that case, you can work through those mistakes together. Do not involve others in the situation, it will only make things blow out of proportion and have other eyes looking sideways at your mate. If you forgive your mate, let it go, bringing it up every time there's a debate won't help the situation. It's enough that we struggle with knowing our own WORTH, much less showing our spouses that they are worthy to us. We take them for granted, assuming they'll always be around, but that is not true. Let's start with learning how to love ourselves unconditionally. Then, we'll understand how to love our spouses unconditionally.

The question to ask yourself, especially those who are not wives, is whether you are playing a wife's role. I would never tell you not to play that role, BUT I would say that being someone's wife and wearing that title is an honor and a gift from GOD. No, it's not always a perfect day. Each day will be different, and you'll learn more about your spouse each day, but you will be growing together, working through any challenge that may arise. Don't play a wife's role when mate does not see himself as your husband. For example, if you're a side piece, his baby momma, or just a friend with benefits. If you're enough to play a wife's role, they must make you their wife. Ladies, demand what you are worth and set boundaries until you receive what you feel you are worth. Honestly, when I was single, I purposely wore a wedding ring, thinking that would keep males from trying to talk to me cause I felt I wasn't in a mental state to be in a relationship. I knew I needed to work on bettering myself first, so I could prepare myself to be able to be in a relationship. And now, even with me being a wife, I'm not perfect. I often fall short in many categories, knowing there are things I should be doing and can do more of but constantly putting them off, and I know for a fact that I work my husband's nerves. Yes, he works mine too, regularly, but I still have expectations of what I feel I'm worth, and of course, those expectations change periodically. As we get older, with the mistakes we both have made, we grow as individuals together, and our expectations will change, which is okay. We have to ensure the changes will better us, and not just unnecessarily expect things.

I frequently catch myself enjoying my time as Rose, trying to take a mental break and going about my day, when I get a phone call or text with an emergency that I have to attend to. One part of me wants to ignore the phone.

Still, the professional and responsible parts in me immediately answers the phone. I handle the situation and return to what I was initially doing, not allowing the disruption to control me. I've learned over time that we must stay in control and remain calm to have a better chance of a positive outcome. When we allow chaos to take charge, we lose control, and that's when the stress creeps in. We have to handle our responsibilities one step at a time. This includes our responsibility to ourselves.

It's funny because I recently met this woman who asked me if I have always been so calm. She said she noticed that I never let things bother or upset me. I smiled at her and stated, "You have no idea." Only God knows that the person I am now isn't who I was a year or two ago. This proved to me once again that someone's always watching you and dissecting you, and you don't even realize it.

Stop:

- Blaming yourself for others' decisions. Free yourself from the weight of responsibility for others' choices. Recognize that you can only control your actions and reactions.

- Second-guessing your words. Release the grip of anxiety over past conversations or remarks. Understand that dwelling on them serves no purpose and hinders your present growth and progress.

- Doubting yourself. Break the cycle of self-doubt and rumination by acknowledging that assigning blame is often unproductive and that focusing on personal growth and forward momentum is more beneficial.

Start:

- Moving on. Embrace self-forgiveness and let go of past mistakes or regrets. Choose to learn from them and forge ahead with confidence and resilience.
- Listening more. Cultivate active listening skills, seek to understand others' perspectives without judgment, and foster deeper connections through attentive and empathetic communication.
- Staying in control. Take ownership of your thoughts, emotions, and actions. Refuse to relinquish control to external circumstances or the opinions of others. Affirm your autonomy and agency in shaping your own life.

Reflective Exercise

Think about a day you felt overwhelmed by the various roles and responsibilities you juggle. Write about how you managed to navigate through your tasks and what strategies you used to stay focused and composed. How did you prioritize your duties, and what did you learn about yourself? Reflect on how maintaining control and balance has impacted your growth and well-being.

CHAPTER 4

Claiming Your Worth

Affirm DIVA!

"I embrace my worth with unwavering confidence and grace. I honor my journey, learn from my past, and refuse to settle for anything less than what I deserve. I am worthy of respect, love, and happiness."

As women, we sit around reminiscing over things we could have done differently and what we don't have. We must learn to be humble and accept what we have instead of competing with others. One of our biggest problems is that we blame ourselves for our past mistakes. We all struggle with something from our past that gives us the feeling that we don't belong, we are not enough, or that people see us differently. Accept who you are and do not allow the judgments and stares to mean there is something wrong with you. Realize they are within that person, and have nothing to do with you. Women somehow choose to accept the harmful abuse, whether it's physical or mental, even knowing inside it's wrong. Then, walk around blaming and second-guessing themselves. We somehow lower our standards to accommodate others, question who we are, and accept so much of what we don't want to keep the peace. We keep a protective shield around us, pretending everything's okay, but knowing we're depressed, unhappy, embarrassed, and always thinking the world knows our wrongdoings and limiting beliefs.

I can think back to a previous relationship where everyone around me saw happiness, but I had lost myself, and I felt there was no return due to being in that space for so many years. Even though I tried mentally on many occasions to leave, I couldn't push myself to do so for some reason. I would work long hours not to go home because I knew whenever I did make it home, it would be a long, unpleasant night, but I knew I wanted and had to go home to my kids. After some people realized what I was going through, they judged me, asking why I stayed in the relationship so long, but until you have enough strength and courage to leave, you stay, thinking things will get better. At one point in my life, I felt as if I was drowning because the abuse was getting more and more stressful and scary. I remember I would be in the kitchen cooking, and the next thing I knew, I would wake up on the floor, where, later on, I found out that my ex had attacked my pressure point, which makes you pass out. Sadly, he never seemed to think performing this on me was a problem. He just felt that it was another way of controlling me. Once I realized what he was doing, I stayed quiet and had minimal conversations to prevent disagreements. I'm now at peace knowing this situation wasn't a lifestyle you're supposed to live but a lifestyle that could have led to significant physical problems. I have now reversed that situation and gained strength when I hear or see water. I no longer feel as if I'm drowning but use water as my therapy to relax.

During a conversation with someone, I was told that their mate chose to have very little to no conversations with them. This triggered a nerve for me due to not being allowed to speak without being called so many terrible names in my previous relationship. A relationship shouldn't be one in which we can only speak when told to speak and not be allowed to discuss certain things that we, as women, may need to say. Unfortunately, that can open your relationship up for total failure and possibly lead you to lean on someone else to talk about those things. They had finally realized they weren't the problem. The other person didn't know how to communicate or couldn't relate to what they were saying to them. They were always in defense mode, knowing that what was being said most of the time was accurate but would never admit it. As people often do, they make you the problem instead of accepting they are the problem. Know your WORTH, and if they don't want to talk to you, let someone else enjoy a conversation with you.

It's their loss. They couldn't take the time to speak to you, hear you, or listen to you. Talking and getting out what's on your mind can be therapy.

Accept YOU. . . Time is too valuable to waste on anyone, and definitely not on a relationship that will go nowhere unless you both are working together. If your mate never asks you what needs to be done, how can they assist you with anything or know what needs to be done within your relationship? Why are you in that relationship? This is another form of settling instead of being involved with a relationship we know is worth it.

I once obtained my dream of becoming a homeowner but gave all that away for the peace of mind of removing myself from a harmful and unsafe relationship. I took a chance of losing my life, but at that point, I was determined it had to be me losing my life or me having peace of mind. I finally grew enough strength to be able to accept that I may lose my life. Still, at that time, I would rather lose my life than continue to live the way I was living and the hurt I was regularly experiencing from an individual who was meant to support, protect, and love me. I gained enough courage to file for a divorce against everything I believed in, but by praying and seeking God to try to understand why and what I was going through, I realized that could not be God''s plan for me. Even though I was trying to separate a vow that was taken, I had to recognize what sense it made to keep claiming a name and title that I despised daily and didn''t want anyone to know I had any affiliation with. I would walk around embarrassed because I could be disrespected with harsh words in public and so many other things that I didn''t even want to go outside of the house sometimes. Sadly, while all this was happening, I was still fluffing my so-called responsibilities to keep peace.

Knowing your worth also means knowing your value as I was put in a situation that I could have lost my freedom and my kids due to illegal activity which I was unaware of. When you love someone, you seem to believe and have faith that what you are being told is the truth and turn your head to things you know are wrong, but until you have proof, it isn''t happening. We lose sight of our worth and put our trust in another individual, not knowing that individual can set us up for failure and possibly accomplish our wrongdoings. We must learn not to ignore signs of things we see going on, good or bad. We must deal with it head-on before it negatively deals with us. We must keep others from being able to determine our next step. We have to be strong enough to say no sometimes and mean it and not just say yes to make things simpler for us.

No, relationships are not perfect, but we as individuals grow and learn each other's do's and don't's. We work on not making the same mistakes and finding ways to work through our differences. To do that, we have to work on ourselves first, then what's needed to prosper as one. If your relationship is just a matter of convenience, perhaps you should move on by yourself until you are able to offer a complete you. Then, find that person who cares about you and what's going on around you. Watch how much you grow with the right person, when you can progress and manifest together.

Yes, when we look back at situations we've allowed to consume us for too long, we regret what we did, but we cannot change the past. We can only acknowledge what happened and demand ourselves to do better next time before it's too late. As a woman and in any relationship, you should have set goals and visions that you work on individually and together. Ladies, God created and designed us the way he wanted us to be, including that we are to be loved and respected. We must know our worth and demand what we are worth. As women, we must understand God created us as he saw fit. Many constantly label us, but most don't take the time to understand.

Some of us are confident in what we do, not arrogant or cocky. The more we grow, the more we will understand our WORTH, not allowing anyone or anything to distract us from that. We must practice what we preach as there are always eyes on us, waiting for us to make the wrong turn. Remember, no one is perfect, and we all make mistakes. You may ask yourself whether I learned from my mistake and whether I will make the same mistake again. I haven't always had this D.I.V.A. mindset, but after going through terrible situations in my life, I finally decided to stop allowing people to use and disrespect me. Once I decided to breathe and let Rose live by any means necessary, my life and health took a significant turn in the right direction. I will continue to walk with my head high and not let negativity consume me. Lately, I'm often asked how I let things roll off like it didn't happen. I smile or laugh, and say that I don't.Don't take this the wrong way. I am available when and if needed, but not for foolishness anymore. Even when someone starts to talk to me about a situation they are having, whether it's personal or business, which I see can be going toward nonsense and drama, I ask, "Is this something I need to know, or can you handle it without me?" I explain that I do not want nonsense in my spirit. I prefer to remain out of it unless you need me to assist. This practice has lowered my blood pressure, and my mind mostly stays free from someone else's issues.

Stop:

- Settling. Break the cycle of accepting less than you deserve in various aspects of your life, whether in relationships, career, or personal growth and commit to pursuing fulfillment and excellence.

- Living in the past. Release the chains of the past that anchor you to regret, resentment, or missed opportunities. Choose to focus on the present moment and its possibilities for growth and transformation.

- Allowing others' issues to affect you. Disentangle yourself from the burden of others' problems or negativity. Recognize that their issues are not yours to carry, and prioritize your emotional well-being and boundaries.

Start:

- Demanding respect. Assert your worth and value, refuse to tolerate disrespect or mistreatment from others, and advocate for yourself with confidence and self-assurance.

- Breathing and living. Embrace each moment with mindfulness and gratitude, taking time to breathe deeply, appreciate the beauty around you, and engage fully in the richness of life.

- Accepting yourself. Practice radical self-acceptance, embrace all aspects of yourself—the strengths, weaknesses, successes, and imperfections—and nurture a deep sense of love and compassion for the unique individual that you are.

Reflective Exercise

Reflect on a time when you settled for less than you deserved, whether in a relationship, job, or personal situation. Write about the moment you realized your worth and decided to change. How did this decision impact your life, and what steps did you take to demand the respect and recognition you deserve? How do you continue to affirm your worth in your daily life?

CHAPTER 5

Leading with Purpose

Affirm DIVA!

"I lead with purpose and determination; understanding my true worth is beyond measure. I invest in myself, empower my team, and stay committed to my vision. I am a leader who inspires and achieves greatness."

As supervisors, we are given policies and procedures that we must follow for the company to flow. These policies and procedures are not our rules, but we are in a position to ensure they are followed. If we are all honest, we regularly ask ourselves if our superiors know our worth and the weight of the responsibilities we have to accomplish. We will never be able to answer that question because there will never be a price tag on any of us that could determine what we are worth. Even if we were to request a higher salary within a period of time, we'd feel that it still isn't what we are worth. I've accepted that my worth isn't a dollar amount; my worth is my peace of mind, as long as I stay in control of the business decisions that I was hired to make.

As we go through the day, we often face many challenges that make us second guess if being ourselves is worth all the nonsense. We also wonder if we're being paid enough to deal with all this nonsense. Of course, we aren't, but we can change that by performing at our highest capability and demanding our worth, whether it is within our current role or a higher role. Will we be someone else's supervisor and make them millions or should we be our own supervisor? We can be our own boss if we trust God's process and stick to God's plan. Ask, and you shall receive.

On the other hand, we as bosses or CEOs sometimes second-guess ourselves because we are the individuals making the decision, thinking about all situations too deeply instead of trusting what our first thought or idea was and going through with it. Each of us can be a boss making boss moves, but we must ensure that whatever we need is accomplished by the boss. As a boss, we've built a team, and we have to remember we are only as good as our team. Build your team and continue to empower them and yourself so everyone wins. Keep your standards high, turn your doubts into planning and developing, and expect excellent outcomes. And we must be mindful of what we are trying to accomplish, realizing that if it doesn't work, it's on us. But we must also realize it's okay cause it was our decision to try. Even if it doesn't work out, we try again until we succeed.

We put so much time and energy into someone else's ideas and help them succeed. Why not put that energy into our own dreams and visions? We wouldn't have anyone standing in our way but ourselves. Let's practice telling ourselves daily, "I Know My Worth." Live by it and motivate yourself until you see results within yourself. We are our own assets and we can invest in ourselves. Investing in yourself means taking chances, and the risk will be ours as well, but we will reap all the benefits, time, and effort.

Stop:

- Allowing daily responsibilities to consume you. Manage your time effectively and prioritize tasks to avoid burnout.

- Hiding behind your flaws. Acknowledge your weaknesses, but don't let them define you. Use them as areas for growth.

- Lowering your standards. Maintain high standards for yourself and your work. Don't compromise on what you deserve.

Start:

- Setting yourself up for success. Plan meticulously, set clear goals, and take proactive steps toward achieving them.
- Following your dreams and vision. Prioritize your aspirations and work diligently toward them.
- Taking ownership of you. Own your decisions, your successes, and your failures. Learn from every experience and grow continuously.

Reflective Exercise

Reflect on a significant leadership decision you've made. What was the situation, and how did you approach the decision-making process? Describe the outcome and the lessons you learned. How do you continue to apply these lessons as a leader today?

CHAPTER 6

Navigating Challenges

Affirm DIVA!

"I am resilient and capable of navigating any challenge that comes my way. I remain calm, composed, and focused, making wise decisions that protect my well-being and drive my success."

Ladies, life happens to us, and we tend to shut down when that happens. We're strong in many ways and always seem to find strength when needed, whether it's our situation or stepping in to help others through theirs. We find ways to be comfortable when required rather than when we want to be. We carry everyone's problems on our shoulders, forgetting there's not much we can do except be an ear for them or talk them through their challenges.

I recall being in a situation at work where I was confronted by a woman who became hostile because I couldn't go into detail about a tenant's confidential issue. My husband and I are both property management professionals, and we had gone to the property together. When we arrived, he left to handle another issue at the property while I went to address a tenant's concern. Upon arriving at the unit, I encountered a woman standing in front of the unit. I asked if she was the tenant, and she replied she was not, then proceeded to demand why I was there. To protect the tenant's privacy, I refused to discuss the matter with her. Instead, I focused on documenting the damage by taking pictures. Despite her rude and offensive remarks, I kept the conversation professional, though it was extremely hard due to what she said. You would think my silence would defuse the situation, but instead, it only inflamed her.

After finishing my task and returning to my vehicle, I noticed a police officer parked behind my car. He exited the car and began questioning me about who I was and what I was doing there. His relentless questions made me feel like I had done something wrong, instead of just doing my job. During this questioning, my husband returned and asked if everything was okay. The officer's focus quickly shifted to him, and the barrage of questions continued. We were both confused and could only look at each other in disbelief.

The officer demanded our licenses and asked us to stay put. My husband's advice to remain calm echoed in my mind. Anyone who knows me will tell you I get very uncomfortable around officers, especially given the current climate where a single misstep can change your life in an instant. I knew that reacting incorrectly could escalate the situation, so I stood there, nervous and upset, waiting for the officer to return our documents.

Looking back, the encounter was a stark reminder that no matter how right we think we are, there's always an enemy ready to distract and derail us. This experience made me question myself and my actions, but I realized it was a test of my resilience and ability to navigate through challenges with grace.

Once we left the site, I discussed it in detail with my husband, who, of course, helped me understand that we cannot control people. We can only control ourselves. This was another wake-up call for me to look at situations differently in the future and make sure the decisions I make do not put me in harm's way or cause unnecessary lifelong personal problems.

Stop:

- Shutting down. Engage with challenges head-on instead of withdrawing.
- Putting yourself in harm's way. Prioritize safety and avoid risky situations.

- Allowing your emotions to control you Stay composed and think clearly in stressful situations.

Start:

- Stepping up. Take proactive steps to address and overcome challenges.
- Thinking more. Strategize and plan effectively before making decisions.
- Making wise decisions. Choose actions that ensure your long-term well-being and success.

Reflective Exercise

Reflect on a recent challenge you faced. How did you respond to it? What strategies did you use to navigate through the situation? Describe the outcome and what you learned from it. How can you apply these lessons to future challenges to ensure better results?

CHAPTER 7

Empowering Others

Affirm DIVA!

"I am deserving of all the good things life
has to offer. I am capable, strong, and resilient.
I believe in myself and my ability to achieve my
dreams. I am enough."

You and I are blessed to have what we have, just a portion of what we all are working toward. Even though we look at our lives and realize they are not perfect, we must always know what we can do to change them for the better. We may not have all we want, but we can do better. We can accomplish whatever we put our minds to, one step at a time. If we want a house, a new car, a new job we must put in the work to get it. We seem so complacent in so many things we do, but if we look deep within ourselves, we are some beautiful individuals with so many talents.

We need that boost to push and keep us going. I challenge you to get up, walk around wherever you may be, and picture yourself in charge, as the owner of wherever you work, whether you're in a restaurant, a grocery store, a department store, or anywhere else. Ask yourself, "Am I at my highest potential?" Of course not. So, let's work on us, let's work toward that dream car you have been wanting, that new house you dream about, that new building you can see yourself setting up for your new business. DREAM, DREAM, DREAM, but turn your dreams into reality one step at a time.

This journey will not be easy, but I've stated in this book that I have been through some challenges in my life, some you wouldn't even imagine. I can finally talk and write about them without them bothering me mentally, and they now inspire me to press forward, looking back at what I needed to live through to be the person I am today. Those challenges gave me the strength to push myself harder to succeed, believing in myself and accepting the sky is the limit to what I can have. The selfish part of me wants to see those individuals who hurt and doubted me, but my spiritual side stays humble, knowing whatever I have and wherever I am in my life can be taken at the drop of a hat. But, no matter what I've accomplished, I will never be satisfied with where I am in life until I have reached my highest potential, which, honestly, I cannot say what that is yet. I need and want generational wealth for my family, and I'm not stopping until I see it manifest.

It could be me making $500 now and $500 billion in the future. I feel it's there for me. So, I'm going for it. Anything and everything is possible if you have faith. I will continue to believe and trust God that soon, all my sowing, hard work, and dedication will pay off, and I'll be able to look back and see I was able to succeed at all the things I wanted to succeed at.

I'm regularly asked how I have so many things going on. When do I sleep and rest? After all, there's only twenty-four hours in a day, right? My response will always be to practice dedicating a minimum of one hour to yourself daily for whatever goals you are working toward. I understand this may be hard sometimes, but you must remain committed to seeing results. My philosophy with my business is I've succeeded as long as I can reach one new client monthly. That one could have been zero, therefore, I'll accept that one until I can turn that one into two, then more.

Stop:

- Feeling like you are undeserving. Embrace your worth and believe in your capabilities.

- Telling yourself you are unqualified. Challenge self-doubt and recognize your potential.

- Thinking you failed. Reframe setbacks as opportunities for growth and learning.

Start:

- Accepting you are enough. Recognize your inherent worth and value.
- Saying you are beautiful inside and out. Affirm your self-worth and embrace your unique beauty.
- Realizing you can achieve anything. Cultivate a mindset of possibility and empowerment.

Reflective Exercise

Reflect on a dream or goal you've been hesitant to pursue. What steps can you take to turn that dream into reality? Identify any limiting beliefs or self-doubt holding you back and challenge them. How can you empower yourself to take action and move closer to your aspirations?

CHAPTER 8

Embracing Self-Care

Affirm DIVA!

"I am worthy of love, respect, and care.
I embrace self-care as a vital part of my journey
to success. I prioritize my well-being
and nurture my mind, body, and soul with compassion and kindness."

This chapter is challenging for me as I am still determining how I would like to write about how I embrace self-care, but being open about my struggles with it might be for the best. With all the things I'm faced with, I tell myself I can and will "Make It Happen." Sometimes, I'm not convinced how to make it happen, but I always seem to do so. I look back at what I've succeeded through but also at significant things I haven't fulfilled which, mentally, is hard for me. Those things, though there aren't many, stay on my mind and will remain until I have accomplished them. As I live and promote self-care, I move in silence when around other people, as everyone I talk to isn't there to encourage me. I'm a believer in the idea that people can pray against you. Over the years, I have learned to love and respect myself, which is how I can work through many obstacles. I will tell people now that I demand my respect as Rose before any other title I have. Some understand, and some don't, but as you grow older, you'll understand all you have is you. Therefore, I will not allow anyone to disrespect me any longer, no matter who that person is. Understand that when you demand your respect, it'll start to come naturally because people around you will see the aura you have on you and won't even attempt to say certain things to you. Yes, they may say crazy things to others about you, but it'll never come directly to you from them. For example, a young lady recently expressed her respect for me. She stated how much she respects who I am as well as me being a woman in the position I'm in. My response was to ensure that if you respect someone, you always show them respect and do not tell them you respect them but speak so negatively about them to others. We were on the phone at this point so I couldn't see her face, but the phone call was quiet for a minute. She responded, "All I can say is that I apologize to you. I was wrong to say anything about you." Ladies, this is just another example of someone always trying to knock you down. See, negativity moves me to push harder. It doesn't affect me or stop me.

Yes, it makes me think why, but I don't allow it to change who I am. Now, imagine if I had reacted poorly to this information I had been aware of for a while. Responding this way was me making sure to help another individual see what she was doing and why she could have now lost the respect she thought she had from someone. I didn't hold it against her, I used that situation to help her realize that this happens to you when you speak negatively about others. Now, the respect she thought she had from others is not there, so I advised her to demand her respect but give respect first and see how things change positively in her life. The older I get, my thought process is I deserve so much more, and not material things. We have purses, clothes, jewelry, and all of those things, but we always feel we deserve much more in many other categories. I can now look in the mirror and see my beauty inside and out. I can finally tell myself I am a queen, that I have whatever it takes to succeed in life and achieve whatever I need to reach my dreams. As my husband states, marry the mirror. Meaning, marry what you see. When you look in the mirror, you should be able to see a reflection of who you are inside and out.

Stop:

- Doubting who you are. Challenge self-doubt and embrace your inherent worth and value.

- Limiting yourself. Replace limiting beliefs with a mindset of abundance and possibility.
- Complaining about others. Shift your focus from negativity to positivity. Foster a more supportive and uplifting environment for yourself.

Start:

- Accepting you are not perfect. Embrace imperfection and recognize that growth comes from learning and evolving.
- Taking time for yourself. Prioritize self-care activities that nourish your mind, body, and soul, promoting overall well-being.
- Helping others see their worth. Empower others to recognize and embrace their inherent value. Foster a culture of positivity and self-love.

Reflective Exercise

Reflect on a time when you neglected self-care in pursuit of other responsibilities or goals. How did this impact your overall well-being? What steps can you take to prioritize self-care moving forward, and how do you envision incorporating self-care practices into your daily life? Consider how embracing self-care can empower you to achieve your goals more effectively and sustainably.

CHAPTER 9

Finding Purpose in Pain

Affirm DIVA!

"I am resilient, and my past pain has shaped me into a stronger, more compassionate individual. I trust in God's plan for my life and believe that every challenge I face has a purpose, guiding me toward greater growth and fulfillment."

Well, ladies, the enemy tried to sneak in again, but let me explain. I went to work with my hubby today to assist him in any way I could on this particular job. It was a very long, challenging day because I was tired from not sleeping as I hadn't felt well the night before. Of course, I didn't share that with my hubby 'cause he would not have gone to this job. As we pulled into the driveway after our long day of work, I had a whole breakdown of how I'm tired of hurting, tired of people who don't know me talking about me, and just venting to my hubby about the things that I'd been going through with my health and daily life in general. I was losing my drive, and the stress was taking control of me. At the end, I ended up telling him I was just tired and got out of the car. He told me that God has brought us through too many things for us to give up on him now. Honestly, I was speechless for some reason and couldn't say anything. I just looked and nodded my head at him. He said to stop allowing people and situations to take control of you or what you're trying to accomplish. He told me, "Remember bae, don't forget your worth." Then he smiled at me and walked away. I really couldn't comment. I just stood there for a minute, then told myself, "Okay." Now inside, I proceeded to get comfortable, but while attempting to do so, I picked up my phone to start my music. There was a notification on the front of my phone, so I opened it up. The notification was a post that a recent speaker I had been following had just posted. When I unmuted it, I heard her say that she had realized her worth and began investing in herself. Yes, she explained in detail what she did, but what sat with me was hearing her say she realized her worth.

To summarize what I assumed she was saying was to stop waiting around, allowing others to knock you down and determine if you are worth anything. You are worth it. Move on from whatever it is and allow God to work through you to show the world what you know you are worth. I shook my head and said, "I hear you." I know God placed that post for me to see and remind me of what he has already confirmed in many ways and situations. I don't always understand why so many things come to me, but my mind always races 100 miles a minute. I wonder why I cannot rest or sleep, but I figure it's because I'm meant to be doing something. I can't seem to figure out what that something is yet, but I try to remain patient to see what's in store for me. Sometimes, it seems like it will take forever.

Today, I will not allow anyone else to have my Joy, Peace, or Happiness. I will not allow any situation control me or my life. I will be obedient, listen to God, and let him use me however he sees fit.

Stop:

- Complaining. Shift your focus from negativity to gratitude. Recognize the blessings in your life despite challenges.
- Allowing others to take your joy. Guard your joy and inner peace against external influences. Choose to find happiness from within.
- Asking for others' validation of you. Seek validation from within rather than relying on external approval. Embrace your inherent worth and value.

Start:

- Accepting God created you. Embrace your unique identity and purpose. Recognize that you are fearfully and wonderfully made.
- Using your inner strength. Tap into your inner resilience and strength to overcome obstacles and persevere through adversity.
- Living one day at a time. Practice mindfulness and presence. Focus on the present moment rather than dwelling on the past or worrying about the future.

Reflective Exercise

Reflect on a time when you experienced pain or adversity in your life. How did this experience shape your perspective or personal growth? Consider how you found strength and purpose in the midst of hardship, and explore any lessons or insights you gained from navigating through challenging times. How can you apply these lessons to empower others in similar situations?

CHAPTER 10

Embracing Your Testimony

Affirm DIVA!

"I am a living testimony of God's grace and mercy. My past challenges have prepared me for my purpose, and I embrace the journey ahead with faith and resilience."

Recently, I had a significant health scare, one which could have cost me my life, and it has opened my eyes once again to see God sending his angels, grace, and mercy over me to keep and protect me. I have no choice but to "Know My Worth" and allow God to lead me in ALL areas of my life. I realize God has continued to keep me on this earth for a reason. I'm not 100 percent sure of the reason, but I assume it may be to motivate others to never give up, continue to push them toward their goals, or trust God and see his miracles happen all around and through me. It touches me sincerely even as I'm writing this, after months of being monitored, making sure I'm doing everything possible to stay focused and maintain a healthy lifestyle in all aspects of my life, to finally be told I am 100 percent blockage-free. I couldn't cry, I couldn't speak, I could only sit still and say, "Thank You, God, for your grace and mercy and saving me once again." But once I got in the car and sat there for a minute and thought about what was just told to me, I accepted it as a message that it's time for me to live, that there's NOTHING that can or will stop me. I realize that many people can't say they made it through significant issues, and I'm sitting here second-guessing myself. This is a new season for me, and I have been released from all BLOCKAGES. I heard God tell me, "My child, stop accepting any and everything and do what your HEART desires. I have repaired/restored your HEART for your new season. Now, go live." I will not die, I will live. No matter what we experience, it's never more than we can handle. Life isn't a game we should be playing roulette with. Life has some significant issues, and without us putting God first and allowing him to lead our walk of life, we will never win. Faith without work is dead. DIVAs, go live. . .

MY TALK (what I say) STARTS MY WALK (walking by faith), WHICH DETERMINES MY SUCCESS. Stop living for approval from others. God already validated who we are. D.I.V.A., ask yourself, do you know your

WORTH? When you can answer that question, you'll be able to live your life to the fullest and know and show the ones you love their WORTH. We must stop doubting our WORTH. We all must understand that it starts within us, and then we can pass it on positively. Imagine if we smiled, laughed, and enjoyed one another more when we are together. It would be amazing. Enjoy life and help others understand their WORTH. Help others understand that they matter. Don't worry about what people say when you walk into the room. Walk confidently, even when all eyes are on you. D.I.V.A., get dressed, put some heels on, walk with your head high, and dominate the room you walk into. Be that confident woman you know you can be, and shine your light brightly. D.I.V.A., wear your crown proudly. Only you and God know your WORTH.

Jeremiah 29:11
"For I know the plans I have for you..."

Stop:

- Living for approval from others. Release the need for external validation and embrace your inherent worth and value.
- Doubting your worth. Recognize that your worth is not determined by others' opinions or standards but by your inherent value as a child of God.

- Ruminating on past struggles. Let go of dwelling on past challenges and instead focus on the present moment and the opportunities ahead.

Start:

- Living life to the fullest. Embrace each day with gratitude and purpose. Know that every moment is a gift from above.
- Empowering others. Share your testimony and uplift those around you. Help them realize their strength and resilience.
- Walking with confidence. Step into your true identity and purpose with confidence. Know that you have a unique and impactful journey.

Reflective Exercise

Reflect on a significant challenge or hardship you've faced in your life. How did you overcome it, and what lessons did you learn from that experience? Consider how your testimony has shaped your identity and purpose, and explore how you can use your story to inspire and uplift others who may be going through similar struggles.

ACKNOWLEDGMENTS

First and foremost, I would like to thank God for continuing to pour into me and for giving me the strength and courage to write this book. This book was therapy for me, as I have faced many challenges. I would have never seen myself open up to write just this little bit, but I was obedient in allowing God to use me to help other women who need to know they are not alone. DIVAs, I love you and wish you success.

I want to thank my husband for being my coach during this journey, supporting and encouraging me, and never allowing me to give up. Thank you for always praying over me and asking God to cover me. Your strength and grace motivate me in many ways to continue to push toward my goals.

To my children, thank you for believing in me and never holding any of my decisions against me. I now understand that I made the decisions I felt were best for all of us at the time.

Never stop believing and trusting God. He will NEVER FAIL YOU.

HELLO TO THE NEW ME…………….. I FINALLY KNOW MY WORTH …………………..

LOVE,
Rose

www.ingramcontent.com/pod-product-compliance
Lightning Source LLC
Chambersburg PA
CBHW070602170426
43201CB00012B/1901